RAISING QUAIL: A COMPREHENSIVE GUIDE TO QUAIL FARMING

Complete Guide on Everything you need to know on Quail keeping and Creating your own farm.

MATHEW JERRY

Copyright © 2024 by Mathew Jerry

All rights reserved. No part of this book/guide may be reproduced, distributed, or transmitted in any way, form or by any means, including photocopying, recording it out, or other electronic or mechanical methods out there, without the prior written permission of the author(Jerry).

About the Author

I, **Mathew Jerry,** is a passionate quail farmer with over 6 years of hands-on experience in raising these remarkable birds(quails). My journey into quail farming began as a backyard part time hobby, but quickly grew into a thriving enterprise as I then discovered the joys and challenges of working with these fascinating creatures.

My dedication to quail husbandry has led me to fully experiment with various breeding techniques, housing set up systems, and feeding regimens. My farm, affectionately known as "Huffy's j Haven," named after his first and most beloved quail, Huffy, has become a model of my efficiency and compassionate animal care in the quail farming community.

This book is the culmination of Mathew's years of hands-on experience, meticulous record-keeping, and passion for quail farming. We wrote it with the sincere desire to help both novice and experienced quail farmers out there.

When not tending to his quail or writing, Me and my family enjoy educating others about sustainable farming practices and the benefits of quail products. We live on our farm with my family and, of course, hundreds of happily clucking quails.

Table of Contents

About the Author 2

Introduction 10

   Why Raise Quail? 10

   Benefits of Quail Farming 13

   Overview of the Book 16

Part I: Getting Started with Quail Raising 19

Chapter 1: Understanding Quail 19

   Quail Species and Varieties 19

   Notable variations include of: 20

   Quail Anatomy and Behavior 21

   Quail Life Cycle 24

   Lifespan Estimate 26

Chapter 2: Setting up the Quail Coop 28

   Coop Requirements and Design 28

   Bedding and Nesting Materials 29

   Feeders and Waterers 31

Chapter 3: Choosing and Acquiring Quail 33

    Selecting the Right Breed 33

    Sourcing Quail (Hatcheries, Breeders, etc.) 35

    Handling and Transporting Quail 39

    Taking Care of Quail 39

    Moving Quail 40

    Holding Up New Arrivals 41

Part II: Quail Care and Management 43

Chapter 4: Feeding Quail 43

    Nutritional Requirements 43

    Feed Types and Formulas 46

    Free-Choice Feeding 48

    Feeding Schedules and Techniques 48

    Feed Ratios 50

Chapter 5: Quail Health and Biosecurity 52

    Common Quail Diseases and Prevention 52

        Bacterial Diseases 52

Viral diseases 53

Quarantine and Biosecurity Measures 55

Protocol for Quarantine 56

First Aid and Treatments 58

Identifying Symptoms 59

Basic First Aid 59

Chapter 6: Breeding and Incubation 63

Quail Reproductive Cycle 63

Mature Sexual Behavior 63

Season of Breeding 64

Mating Patterns 64

Production of Eggs 65

Setting Up a Breeding Program 65

Pens for Breeding and Ratios 66

Setting Up for Breeding Season 67

Gathering Eggs and Maintaining Records 68

Incubating and Hatching Quail Eggs 69

Configuring an Incubator 69

Managing and Positioning Eggs 70

Duration of Incubation 71

Dealing with eggs 72

Eggs on the Table for Ingestion 73

Equipment for Handling Eggs 73

Features of Quail egg 74

Profile of Nutrition 75

Taste and Adaptability 76

Part III: Advanced Quail Farming 78

CHAPTER 7: Housing and Facility Design 78

Large-scale Quail Housing Systems 78

Ventilation, Lighting, and Climate Control 81

Automation and Technology Integration 84

Gathering and Managing Eggs 86

CHAPTER 8: Quail Product Processing and Marketing 88

Quail Meat and Egg Processing 88

Egg Processing 89

Grading and Packaging.. 89

Strategies for Marketing and Sales 90

CHAPTER 9: Management of Quail Enterprises 92

Budgeting and Financial Planning 92

Initial Expenses 92

Budgeting for Operations 93

Maintaining Records and Documentation................... 94

Rules and Legal 95

Part IV: Appendices.. 97

Appendix A: Quail Breed Profiles 97

Appendix B: Formulations for Quail Feed 98

Appendix C: A Guide to Quail Health and Illnesses .. 99

Part V: Expert Quail Production 100

CHAPTER 10: Systems for Farming Quail 100

Pasture- and Free-Range Quail 100

Rules & Licensure 102

Farming Quail Organically 103

Requirements for an Organic System........................104

Procedure for Organic Certification..........................106

Quail-Crop Systems Integrated.................................107

Rules and Certifications for Quail Farming 108

Label Claims and Certifications................................110

CHAPTER 11: Management of Quail Enterprises 112

Budgeting and Financial Planning 112

Budgeting for Operations 113

Introduction

Why Raise Quail?

Growing in recent year's popularity is quail farming, for both commercial producers and small-scale enthusiasts. Growing quail is quite an appealing choice for anyone who wants to practice or grow sustainable agriculture, be self-sufficient, or even simply have a distinctive pet of its own since it has so many advantages.

Quail are very good at turning feed into meat and eggs when being farmed or trained. They develop very quickly, take up little room in your house, and may begin laying eggs as early as 6(six) or 8(eight) weeks of age, during our years with different animals quails are the perfect option for those with limited funds or living house space.

One may grow each quail for their eggs, meat, or even both. They have very healthy, tasty, and lean meat to get, and their eggs are full of strong protein and have a unique flavor that many people would like. In contrast to other poultry species you can get, quail need less upkeep/maintenance as they are resilient and disease-resistant, quiet and simple to maintain in the house, and don't need big coops or runs.

For kids in particular, raising quail around a child's environment will be a very beneficial educational experience as they develop and grow. It will be a fulfilling family pastime and fosters a respect for small animals or animals in general and the food production process.

A sustainable method or pattern that we have tried and know that it can support regional food systems and self-sufficiency is **quail farming**. Raising quail can be easy as raising them on leftover food from your kitchen and other easily accessible feed source requires little effort to make or get.

Now we know Quail are kept mostly for their body meat and eggs, but they can actually make interesting and fun pets to be around. They are a distinctive alternative to conventional home type pets because of their tiny body size, intriguing activities, and very minimal given care requirements.

Whether you are interested in them for their culinary worth, educational giving potential, or just as an intriguing pastime. We'll go over everything you need to know to begin quail farming and taking care of them in the next chapters ahead, including house setup, breeding, maintenance, management and lots more.

Benefits of Quail Farming

A variety of advantages make quail farming a desirable endeavor for both commercial use and small-scale enterprises. The following are some of the main benefits of quail raising we have gathered over the years:

Low Start-Up Costs: The initial expenditure needed for quail farming is very less when compared to other livestock species owning. Since the birds themselves don't need a lot or too much of housing or equipment, it's a viable choice for those on a tight budget.

Only a few square feet of living area/space are required for each bird kept there . Because of this, quail farming is a practical choice for those with small backyards or plots of land to build a home for them.

Quick Maturity and Production: In as little as 6 to 8 weeks of growing, quail may reach slaughter weight. As early as six weeks of age, females can even start producing eggs themselves, offering a quick return on investment.

High Feed Conversion Ratio: Quail have a very high feed-to-meat and egg conversion rate to give back to you. They have one of the finest feed conversion ratios of any species of chicken out there, which lowers input costs and makes them more affordable to produce.

Disease Resistance: In general, quail are resilient as said and resistant to a wide range of typical poultry common illnesses. This lessens the chance of disease outbreaks that can easily wipe out bigger flocks and lessens the requirement for intensive veterinarian care.

Versatile Products: Products gotten from quail farming include good meat, eggs, and even manure-based fertilizer from their waste. Value-added product prospects and numerous revenue streams from them are made possible by this diversification.

Minimal Environmental Impact: The environmental impact of quail farming is minimal, so you don't have to be so much worried about your environment. Compared to bigger cattle or even some chickens, the birds use less resources, generate less waste to handle, and may even be included into sustainable agricultural systems.

Recreational and instructive Value: Teaching your kids about animal husbandry, food production, and responsibility via quail farming would be a fun and instructive experience with them.

For individuals looking for a profitable, efficient, and fulfilling agricultural endeavor to start with or invest in, quail farming offers a lot of advantages and is thus a desirable option to go for , whether one is farming for just personal or commercial gain.

Overview of the Book

The goal of this in-depth manual is to provide quail farmers or yet to be farmers, regardless of experience level you have , the fundamental information and useful skills they need to raise their quail successfully.

Section I: Beginning the Process of Raising Quail

The foundations of quail farming are covered in this part of the book, including knowledge of the anatomy, quail behavior, and life cycle of quails. It walks you the readers through the process of building a functional coop (housing space), selecting the ideal breed of quail to go with, and obtaining and caring for the birds.

Section II: Management and Care of Quails

You can then discover comprehensive information on how to give your quail flock the best care possible right here. Topics covered include appropriate offered nutrition, first aid, common illness treatments/prevention, and quail health maintenance via biosecurity controls. This section also explores quail incubation practice and breeding methods.

Section III: Expert Quail Production

This section examines large-scale quail housing systems, facility design factors including lighting and ventilation, and the incorporation of automation technology for your farm looking to expand their business. Aspects of corporate management, marketing tactics, and quail product processing are also covered in this part.

Section IV: Appendices

Additional resources for learning about quail general health and diseases, breed profiles, feed formulation guidelines, incubation troubleshooting suggestions, and a short list of useful references are included in this other section.

You'll find helpful tips, detailed and easy instructions, and real-world examples all throughout the book to guide you through every phase of quail farming, from starting a small home flock to running a profitable commercial quail business of your own.

Part I: Getting Started with Quail Raising

Chapter 1: Understanding Quail

Quail Species and Varieties

There are really over 100(hundred) distinct kinds of quail in the globe, despite the fact that the name "quail" is often used to refer to only one kind of bird. Only a few species, nevertheless, are often bred for their flesh, eggs, or as pets or avian birds. The following are a few of the most well-liked species and types of quail we have worked with over the years:

Coturnix Quail (Coturnix coturnix): This species is most often bred for just domestication and farming. The most popular kind of coturnix farmed for body meat and eggs is the Japanese or Pharaoh Quail that is renowned for their quick development and prolific egg-laying.

Tuxedo/English White: Features tuxedo-like markings in either black and white with a popular decorative variety.

Texas A&M/Jumbo Brown: A larger breed designed to provide more body meat.

Colinus virginianus, the Bobwhite Quail
Bobwhites are another species native to the North America region that are often reared for game bird hunting and release initiatives.

Notable variations include of:

Native to the eastern United States, the Eastern/Northern Bobwhite

Western/Masked Bobwhite: Found in Mexico and the southern United States

Native to Florida, the Florida/Black-Breasted Bobwhite subspecies

Oreortyx pictus, a smaller species of quail native to North America, with intricate light feather pattern and are quite challenging to raise in a confinement.

Button Quail (Turnicidae family: many species) Small, ground-dwelling quail maintained as fascinating pets or aviaries.

Quail Anatomy and Behavior

- **Anatomy**

Even though they are little, quail have several distinctive anatomical characteristics to look out for.

Skeletal System: Quail have hollow type bones in their skeletal system, which makes them strong and lightweight and enables flight for short periods. They also have very resilient beaks and long out skulls.

Digestive System: Quail, like other fowl-like animals, have a crop that serves as a temporary food storage area before the food is ground and digested in the gizzard.

The respiratory system of quail allows for effective oxygen supply or flow and respiration via the use of lungs and body air sacs.

Feathers: The plumage of quail birds is made up of strong/firm flying feathers and soft contour feathers for insulation and waterproofing (weather conditions). Age and species might have different molt patterns where the feathers drop.

Legs and Feet: Quail, for the most part, have scaly like feet with four toes apiece, which are useful for them running, scratching, and perching on hard surfaces.

- **Behavior**

Quail reside better in family or covey groupings that are clearly divided into social classes. Males are known to be territorial, while hens are often more submissive.

Nesting and Breeding: Before being broody, hens can lay many eggs in just a single clutch and construct basic ground nests by themselves. Male call patterns or noises are used to entice females during breeding sessions.

Feeding: Quail are nature foragers on the ground, picking at seeds, greens, and insects with their sharp beaks, while feeding them it is important to add grit to help digestion.

Activity Patterns: Quail spend the hot midday hours (12-2pm) resting in covered locations, and they are most seen active in the early morning and evening.

Quail Life Cycle

Here's a summary of the major life stages of quails:

Egg Stage: Before hatching, quail eggs must incubate for around 15 to 18 days. It's crucial to maintain the right humidity level and temperature at this sensitive stage.

Incubation (0–4 weeks)
Quail chicks that hatch under the warmth of a brooder are known as precocial, meaning that they

are fully coated in downy feathers at birth and can walk and feed themselves very quickly as they grow, thus stage in growth calls for a particular chick diet.

Juvenile/Growing (4-6 weeks)

Chicks start to gain weight and develop their juvenile light feathers quickly. Giving them the best nourishment or feed possible at this crucial juncture will help them grow better into healthy, productive adult quails.

Pullet/Cockerel (6-8 weeks)

The plumage of male and female quail will be easily distinguished from one another at this phase. During this stage, young females known as pullets will start depositing their first full eggs.

Adult Quail (8 weeks)

At eight weeks old, quail reach full sexual maturity and are regarded as adults. While males engage in full courting and breeding rituals with females, hens will consistently deposit eggs in their nest.

Peak Egg Production: 4-8 months

Between the ages of 4 and 8 months, female quail are most prolific, with a maximum of around 200-300 eggs lay at this time, afterwards the quantity of eggs rapidly decreases after that.

Retiring or eliminating (12+ months)

Upon reaching their first year of daily operation, the majority of commercial quail businesses begin to cull or prepare birds for meat advantage.

Lifespan Estimate

Coturnix quail can solely survive for two to three years if given the right care, but most commercially used birds are killed before they reach their full growing potential.

Chapter 2: Setting up the Quail Coop

Coop Requirements and Design

Quail coops don't have to be very big or intricate buildings, but they do need to meet a few standards; Give each adult bird at least 0.5 to about 1 square foot in space, to avoid the problems of congestion, more space is preferable. In order to enable quail to stand comfortably erect, coops height should be at least 12 to 16 inches up high with good protection that shields them from hawks, snakes, and rats (we advise using Welded wire mesh of at least ½).

Ventilation: Adequate air movement and flow is essential to fix for them , this can be done by providing vents in the coop's upper and lower regions, the home temperature of 60–80°F range is good. Add doors and apertures that are human-sized to facilitate simple and easy cleaning, egg gathering, etc.

Materials to Use: Metal and wood are typical materials, these are reasonably priced choices to build with. Steer clear of things that might or can harm your birds or are hazardous.

An ideal coop has distinct spaces for sleeping, eating area, laying eggs, and even taking dust baths in addition to the standard strong covers.

Bedding and Nesting Materials

For quail to remain healthy and productive, the right bedding and nests are essential, we would detail the materials for each and how we use them in our farm:

- Bedding

To make cleaning more easier, place 2-4 inches of absorbent type bedding, like wood cut shavings or straw, on the coop floor.

- Nesting Boxes

For them to lay eggs and it doesn't get damaged, each five should have a minimum of one 12 by 12" nesting box placed around the corner. Cover with sphagnum moss or bedding.

- plants for Nests

Fragrant plants, such as lavender, may promote the building of nests.

- Material Depth

To allow for digging, keep 4-6 inches of bedding depth in nest boxes.

___Feeders and Waterers___

- Waterers and Feeders

Quail housing layout should have a plastic food area, like plates which should serve as appropriate feeders and waterers:

- Feeders

To reduce waste around, use feeders with straight sides. Frequently change the feed if not eaten within the first few hours of giving them to prevent spoiling.

- Waterers

Fresh, clear water is a must for quail diet and feeding. We advise you to get waterers for poultry or drip systems.

- Positioning

To minimize food and water soiling, raise feeders and waterers up a little.

Chapter 3: Choosing and Acquiring Quail

Selecting the Right Breed

Pharaoh or Japanese quail

This is the most popular coturnix type grown globally, valued for its outstanding ability to produce both eggs and meat for its owners with good care:

- Eggs: At their prime, hens may lay as many as 250-300 eggs annually.

Meat: In about 6-7 weeks, they start to reach a slaughter weight of 5–6 oz.

- Reliable fast producers throughout many laying cycles

English White Quail (Tuxedo)

a kind of decorative coturnix distinguished by its unusual thick black and white plumage:

- Mainly kept for show or as pets because of their beauty in body

Good layers, but not as prolific as the other Japanese quail;-Usually smaller than the production strains in terms of its all body size

Texas A&M/Jumbo Brown Quail

Developed for higher body weight via line breeding:

- One of the biggest coturnix kinds, weighing about 8 to 10 oz when fully grown
- They are Outstanding meat producers, but mediocre egg production
- May not be as resilient to heat or humidity as Japanese type quail

Other possible breeds out there to think about include the distinctive Button quail species for aviaries or pets, or the Bobwhite quail for hunting.

Consider your own priorities while choosing your breed: what is more essential in the process, producing the most eggs or meat? Or would you want a bird with two uses? Think about the environment as well, because some breeds are more suited to extreme heat or cold than others. You may create a flock from the beginning that is tailored to your unique quail farming objectives by carefully choosing and considering the breeds. **The next section looks at trustworthy places to purchase your foundation breeding stock.**

Sourcing Quail (Hatcheries, Breeders, etc.)

Getting your foundation flock or viable hatching eggs is the next step after choosing the breed of quail you want to start with. There are several choices on where to find or get a quail for yourself:

- Hatcheries

A practical way to get day-old chicks or eggs for home incubation is via quail hatcheries. Advantages of using hatcheries consist of:

- A large assortment of breeds, including speciality in types
- Consistent supply from respectable, accredited sources
- The capacity to order the exact amounts required
- Measures for quality control and health testing

Nevertheless, compared to other sources you can try, buying from hatcheries does come at a greater cost per chick you acquire.

- Nearby breeders

Small-scale quail breeders that sell directly to the public may be found in many places or farms. This might be a more reasonably priced choice with advantages like:

- Well-established, locally tailored breeding lines
- The chance to see buildings and birds up close
- Practical guidance from knowledgeable breeders
- Reduced pay/expenses by cutting down on shipping

The main drawbacks, in contrast to hatcheries, are potentially greater biosecurity hazards and a mostly restricted selection of breeds.

- Internet Resources

Additionally, there are a ton of internet quail breeders out there and auction sites that provide countrywide bird shipping. Even if it's easy to just get one from there, purchase with caution because you never can tell who are unreliable or unregistered suppliers.

- Sales/Trades

Seasonally, local farm shops, auctions arenas, and poultry exchanges sometimes have animal stock available in which you can find quails there to get. While this may result in favorable negotiations, it also raises biosecurity issues.

Always ask for paperwork about their hatch dates, full health tests, and any treatments given when sourcing quail to take home. It is also very recommended that new immigrants or adopted quails be properly quarantined before adding to other quails.

To rapidly develop your own viable egg production, it is typically advised that you obtain mature trios (two hens[females] and one male) from a reputable breeder or hatchery for your first set flock.

Handling and Transporting Quail

Even though they are a robust type bird, quail still need to be handled carefully while being caught, moved, and transported. Using the right procedures reduces the birds' stress and any potential damage.

Taking Care of Quail

Quail need a gentle light touch while handled because of their tiny stature and propensity to startle very easily:

To prevent your quail from hurting themselves, move slowly and calmly when coming around them especially if you have a large flock of them. Gently scoop up the birds, holding them in your hands without squeezing them. Fully supporting their bodies, keeping in mind their fragile bones, these birds need soft handling to as little as possible to reduce stress. When you grasp them , throw , carry them by the legs or wings, or let their heads dangle down can hurt them.

Moving Quail

Provide suitable air flow containers when transporting quail over short distances or sending them via carriers when traveling or taking them home:

- Make use of airtight plastic or smooth wood containers.
- For security and to minimize light exposure, cover one-third to one-half of the container.
- Use bedding to line containers to absorb moisture and prevent piles-ups

- Secure containers to prevent moving and give thick bedding for vehicle transit; - Allocate at least one square foot of floor space for five to six adult quail to prevent crowding.
- When shipping, make sure to properly identify containers with the contents and the delivery details. - Try to avoid sending quail during periods of excessive heat.

Stress, injuries, and possible quail losses during handling and shipping can be quite decreased by using the proper equipment and adopting preventative measures in the journey.

Holding Up New Arrivals

Before reintroducing freshly bought quail to an established flock, it is imperative to quarantine them for a minimum of 25-30 days, regardless of whether they are adults, chicks, or even hatching eggs, by doing this practice any possible disease transmission is prevented.

Part II: Quail Care and Management

Chapter 4: Feeding Quail

Nutritional Requirements

Quail, like other birds, need a balanced diet rich in certain nutrients for healthy development, quality egg production, and general wellbeing. Creating the best feeding regimen for them requires an understanding of their nutritional requirements which we would take you through on this part of the guide.

- Proteins

Quail body development, egg production, and feathering all depend on proteins given to them as they grow. 24-29% protein levels are necessary:

- Chicks (0–6 weeks): 28% protein to promote quick and healthy growth

- Pullets/Cockbirds: 24-26% protein (6–20 weeks)
- Laying Hens: 26-28% protein to sustain the production of quality eggs
- Breeders: 28–30 percent protein for hatchability and strong fertility

- Energy

Quail have high metabolic rates and rely more on lipids and carbs to meet their energy demands.
- Growing birds: metabolizable energy of 2,800–3,000 kcal/kg
Levels: 2,800–2,900 kcal/kg of energy that can be easily metabolized
Usually provided by cereals, oils, and bird supplements

- Calcium

Essential for the firm development of eggshells and strong bones:

- Laying hens: oyster shell and limestone supply 2.5–3.5% of the calcium needed while growing.
- Without layers: 0.6-0.9% calcium is enough

- Minerals and Vitamins

Minerals including phosphorus, manganese, and zinc are also necessary and essential in their diet. Vitamin A is needed for sharp eyesight, reproduction, and immunological function. Vitamin D is needed for calcium/phosphorus absorption and bird bone calcification. Vitamin E is an antioxidant that is necessary for better fertility and hatchability.

Although quail are effective feed converters, various life stages nevertheless need varying nutritional balances and levels. Deficiencies do have a negative effect on your bird's health, growth, and all time productivity.

Feed Types and Formulas

Commercially Prepared Rations

Many commercial meals that are nutritionally adequate and tailored for certain development stages are used by quail raisers for proven convenience.

Initial Meal (0–6 weeks)
- 2.5% calcium, 28–30% protein
- In pellet or crumble like shape
- For young quail that have just hatched

Feed for Growers (6–20 weeks)
- Protein content, should be 24-26%
- Given to them in Mash or pellet form

20+ week Layer Feed
- 25% calcium, 2.5–3% protein

- Crumble or mash the texture
- To maximize the production of good eggs

Breeder Feed: Increases overall hatchability and fertility with 25% protein and high calcium content in the feed.

Mixes and Rations at Home

A cost-effective solution for small flocks is to make your own whole rations from separate ingredients:

Example Layer Ratio:

- 40% maize
- 30 percent soybean meal
- 20% middling's of wheat feed
- 6.5% calcium source; 5% fishmeal
- 3.5% mineral/vitamin premix

When combined appropriately, this offers them around 20% protein and satisfies other important dietary requirements for your layers.

Free-Choice Feeding

Some quail owners I've seen choose to give their bird's free-choice from a variety of nutritional sources rather than full diets.

- Whole grains such as oats, maize, and wheat
- Concentrates of proteins (fishmeal or soybean)
- Sources of calcium (limestone or oyster shells)

Supplements premixed with both vitamins and minerals

Tip: Use fresh, premium ingredients and always offer clean ready water, regardless of the feed method being utilized with them. It's also crucial to store feed properly out of dust or dirt and clean feeders often.

Feeding Schedules and Techniques

Feeding Schedules

Chicks (birth to six weeks)

Provide chicks with free access to water and chick starter feed, each extra feedings should be distributed four(4) times a day for the first two(2) weeks then from three to six weeks, switch to two to three feedings a day.

Cockbirds/pullets (6–20 weeks)
- Free access to water and grower feed
- Advice you offer meal feeding once or twice a day

Laying Hens: - Distribute meals in the morning and afternoon while allowing unrestricted access to water and layer feed.

Breeding Flock (male and female): - Unrestricted access to water and layer breeder feed should be provided but also offer light meal feeding to maintain condition.

Feed Ratios

Observe these general feeding recommendations depending on age and purpose:

- Growers

15–25 grams per bird per day, depending on size grown to

- Chicks

Unlimited feed for the first two(2) weeks, after which each chick will get 7–10 grams.

- Layers

Each bird should get 20–35 grams of layer feed every day. Breeders should match layer levels to ensure sound optimal health.

To modify their diets appropriately, keep an eye on your flock consumption and body weights.

Feeders

Feed waste is decreased by well-designed feeders:
- Make use of tube or troughs with catch lips.

- Give each adult bird 3—4 inches of feeder space; - Hang tube feeders off of litter to maintain clean given feed

- Frequently clean and replenish all feeders with new food after a few hours of giving them.

Supplements

Moreover, your quail could benefit from getting extra supplementation:

- Layers of oyster shell or limestone powdered grit
- Fresh greens, such as alfalfa or vegetable chopped leftovers, just make sure the supplements with vitamins and electrolytes, pelleted as required

Chapter 5: Quail Health and Biosecurity

Common Quail Diseases and Prevention

Quail are hardy type birds, yet they can become sick or ill from a variety of parasitic, bacterial, and viral infections common to them. Preventive measures and raising awareness are quite crucial for maintaining your flock's health.

Bacterial Diseases

Ulcerative Enteritis, caused by Clostridium bacterium, affects the digestive tract of the birds. Among the common symptoms include diarrhea, dehydration, and constant weight loss in your quail. As preventive measures to this, avoid overcrowding, clean space thoroughly, and use antibiotics sparingly.

Cholera is a highly contagious bacterial sickness not just in humans but quails that are acquired by giving them contaminated food or drink which causes steady drowsiness, ruffled feathers, and greenish diarrhea. In endemic areas, biosecurity, rodent control, and vaccination are preventative measures to this.

Viral diseases

"Quail bronchitis" is the name of the disease that can solely cause respiratory issues such as coughing, slow gasping, and quail nasal discharge can hinder the growth of your young bird.

Avoidance compliance with strict biosecurity and good hygiene protocols are ways to prevent this.

Newcastle disease is a paramyxovirus that affects the quail's whole nerve system. Among the symptoms are paralysis, circling, and twisted looking necks.

Take caution: very contagious to others ; swiftly segregate and eliminate any affected bird(s).

Problems with Fungi and Parasites

The Eimeria parasite that causes coccidiosis may cause bloody diarrhea, dehydration, and fast stunted growth if treatment from the vet is not received.

Preventive measures include switching up living quarters, keeping things around clean, and adding coccidiostats to their food.

Aspergillosis

This fungal-related respiratory illness is known to be brought on by moldy bedding or feed and it causes gasping, rapid appetite loss, and even weight loss.

Prevention: Take good care of your bird's bedding to avoid any moisture accumulation.

External Parasites

Lice, mites, and other parasite infestations can cause them skin irritation, anemia, and reduced productivity in your quail.

Preventive measures include frequently cleaning the area/space around the coop and using pesticide treatments that are safe for your birds.

The best defense for any common illness is prevention in the form of preventive biosecurity measures such as proper balanced diet, full home ventilation, overpopulation control, and general hygiene.

Quarantine and Biosecurity Measures

Strong biosecurity procedures must be put in place, such as appropriate new arrival quarantine, in order to stop any illnesses from entering and spreading throughout your existing quail flock. Note that

Pathogens can even be carried by birds that seem healthy so don't be fooled by a happy playing quail.

Protocol for Quarantine

Before permitting interaction with the current population at hand , any new quail—day-old chicks, hatching eggs, or adult birds; should all be fully quarantined:

Use specific attire around the house, shoes, boots, tools, and equipment for quarantine, separate the quarantine facilities you made from main coops while Isolate all new arrivals in a separate quarantine pen/brooder for a minimum of 25-30 days. While they are quarantined keep a close eye on them while you observe if there are any indications of sickness in isolated quail

Hatched eggs from unknown sources should be kept in a quarantined incubator, these procedures should only be done if there are established flocks. If illness then arises during this phase, prolong the quarantine time appropriately. When the quarantine then goes well and there are no health problems, you can then safely reintegrate the newly gotten quail into the main existing flock.

Broad Biosecurity

In addition to quarantine phase , additional crucial biosecurity procedures are also involved:

1. Limit traveler and car access to your quail regions in order to prevent the spread of illness.
2. Place disinfecting type footbaths and boot baths at each entry to their space.
3. Maintain "all-in, all-out" flock management by:
   - regular Cleaning and disinfecting drinkers, feeders, and coop spaces

4. Prevent your quail from coming into touch with other poultry or wild birds if you own one or have one around.
5. Dispose of any dead birds if you get one in the flock and waste materials properly.
6. Keep up a rodent and pest control program(at least twice a week).
7. Set up a thorough cleaning and disinfection routine in between flock cycles.

First Aid and Treatments

Even with our greatest precautions to them , our quail still becomes sick or gets injuries that need professional medical attention. For afflicted birds in your flock , knowing how to identify these signs and provide the right care might be the difference between good life and saving from death.

Identifying Symptoms

Since early diagnosis is quite crucial, keep an eye out for any symptoms of sickness in your flock, symptoms you would see or notice are—-

- Slumbering in a corner
- A noticeable fast decrease in appetite or weight
- Unusual breathing pattern or nasal discharge
- Untidy or rumpled like feathers
- Bloodstains and diarrhea in the vent region
- Lameness or other visible injuries
- Odd body positions in the coop or neurological symptoms

Basic First Aid

Basic first aid care are for small wounds or wounds that are prior to veterinary care——

Wound Care

Use betadine or chlorhexidine to clean and disinfect any seen wounds or abrasions. Put on light bandages and antibacterial ointment as necessary in the wound area.

Dehydration

If the quail is conscious and able to swallow, provide electrolyte solutions using an eye dropper or small clean dish. Offer small hydrating fruits and vegetables as a remedy as well.

Isolation

Take ill quail and place them in a warm, cozy, hygienic area where they can be easily observed and given treatment they need, if Isolation done correctly stops flock spread of ant disease.

Treatment

Treatments that are known to be suitable for certain ailments or diseases (note we have personally tested all this)

Antibiotics: For bacterial illnesses such as cholera or ulcerative enteritis. To prevent resistance, medication must be given steady and taken carefully.

Anti-parasitics: insecticides and dewormers for both internal and external parasites in your quails. To stop resistance, switch up the medication classes.

Probiotics and prebiotics: To help the gut microbiota recover from antibiotic treatment or illness obstacles.

Electrolytes and vitamins: Promote them healing from illnesses, trauma, anxiety, or periods of dehydration.

Pain Relievers: Meloxicam and other anti-inflammatories should be used sparingly to minimize any pain in your bird while healing.

For severe or unresolved health conditions, especially highly infectious illnesses needing strong treatment methods, seeking expert veterinarian care is fully advised.

Chapter 6: Breeding and Incubation

Quail Reproductive Cycle

A thorough understanding of quail reproduction is necessary for profitable breeding operations. Even though quail have a quicker reproductive cycle than chickens, they still need the right circumstances for successful mating, egg formation, and fertilization.

Mature Sexual Behavior

Coturnix quail mature sexually rather quickly.
- Females (pullets) do start producing eggs as early as 6 weeks of age
- Males (cockerels) mature between 6 and 8 weeks growing

Season of Breeding

Unlike many other birds out there, quail can solely reproduce all year long as long as the right climatic parameters are satisfied, without following a set seasonal pattern:

- Adequate temperatures between 70 and 80°F - 14 to 17 hours of light every day promotes fertility in females with an abundance of high-protein food and calcium intake

Mating Patterns

Male quail engage in courting displays, which include circling around females, neck strutting, and vocalizing different mating sounds to them, in order to begin reproducing.

- Female coveys depart to construct their own nests on grass-lined terrain.
- Hens spend about 16–18 days incubating clutches of 8–12 eggs after mating with males.

Production of Eggs

When circumstances are right, female quail have amazing capacity for better reproduction:
Capable of producing up to 250-300 eggs annually in their prime age which is most prolific between the ages of 4 and 8 months
- Give them a 9-14-day rest after every clutch cycle before starting new again with egg-laying.

During the mating season, the fertility rate is greatest in housing trios of one male and two female quail.

To enhance the reproductive effectiveness of your quail, use proper flock management strategies such as providing nest boxes, controlling light cycles, and using tested breeding ratios.

Setting Up a Breeding Program

You may maximize your breeding production by using certain tactics after you have a thorough grasp of the quail reproductive cycle. It is crucial to organize and manage breeding activities properly.

Pens for Breeding and Ratios

Even while quail may be produced as a single, cohesive flock, individual breeding cages provide for better oversight and management:

- Provide each bird in breeding pens at least 2 square feet of room.
- House breeding trios of 1 male and 2 female together per pen area.
- Ensure that enclosures provide water, feeders, places for nesting, and covered roosts.
- Clearly mark the birds in each pen so that breeding records may be made.

In order to enhance reproductive rates and avoid excessive male rivalry or harassment of hens, it is desirable to maintain a 1:2 male to female ratio.

Setting Up for Breeding Season

Simulate springtime circumstances to initiate and maintain reproductive conditioning:
- Use timed lighting to extend the day to 16–17 hours - Try to keep temperatures between 70 and 80°F - Switch to a higher 28% protein breeder feed diet - Give hens extra calcium sources, such as oyster shells

- Nest Boxes

Give them plenty of space to nest and specialized nest boxes so they may lay eggs:

- 12" by 12" wooden or plastic nest boxes are effective; - Add 4-6 inches of wood shavings or other nesting litter.

Place boxes 12–14 inches above the ground. Permit one nest box to be accessed by each two-three hens.

Dried lavender is one of the herbs that may be used to stimulate nesting behavior.

Gathering Eggs and Maintaining Records

Gather eggs from nest boxes two to three times a day when production is at it's all highest , then Label and store viable hatching eggs with the pointy end facing downward. Keep a breeding journal at side that records hatch rates, egg counts, bird rotations, etc.

You may easily generate viable hatching eggs for more incubation and flock propagation all year long with careful preparation and attention to the environmental management.

Incubating and Hatching Quail Eggs

For optimal embryonic development and excellent hatch rates from them, the incubation phase is essential after obtaining viable eggs from your the breeding program. Particular conditions for temperature, humidity, and turning are necessary for quail eggs to hatch well.

Configuring an Incubator

Still-air incubators with automated rotation capabilities are what is used in the majority of quail enterprises. Considerable features include:

Temperature: Throughout the incubation time, keep the temperature between 99.5 and 100°F in there.

Relative humidity of 50–55% is excellent up to lockdown, when it should be 84–90%.

Autonomously rotating every one to two hours fully ensures that embryos remain correctly orientated.

Airflow: Light airflow is very good, but keep breezes away from your eggs directly.

NOTE: Hatchability is increased and contamination is duly reduced by cleaning the whole incubator and employing a hygiene air filter.

Managing and Positioning Eggs

Lay eggs horizontally in incubator trays or racks;- Collect eggs two(2) to three(3) times a day;-Store pointed end down at 55 to 65°F;-Allow gathered eggs to warm up before placing them in incubator gradually;-Start slowly turning and monitoring the incubation period after all eggs are then placed.

Duration of Incubation

The incubation time for Coturnix quail is typically about 16–18 days. Chicks will hatch 16–18 days after each setting, then a lockdown at 15 days to promote quality humidity for hatching. Stop automated turning in last 3(three) days as embryos position to pip. The time hatch window for 24 hours to provide straggler eggs enough time to hatch

After the eggs are totally dry, transport them to a brooder at 98°F with feed and clean water. Candle any unhatched eggs after 20-24 hours to remove any rotten or halted embryos. Leave the hatcher for 12 to 24 hours to fluff up and extract the remaining chicks out.

Dealing with eggs

Proper egg handling is essential whether your objective is to produce eggs for consumption or to hatch viable eggs to support your breeding flock. Ensuring optimal hatchability and egg quality is facilitated by meticulous egg collecting, washing, and storage.

To hatch eggs, follow these guidelines:
• Gather viable eggs from nest boxes two to three times a day during the busiest times of the year
• Prevent undue jarring, rolling, or even temperature swings
• Gently remove any dirt or debris with a dry light cloth
• Store eggs pointed end down in a clean carton or flat at 55 to 65°F and 75% percent humidity
• Set eggs for incubation time within seven to ten days for optimal hatchability

- Throw away any cracked, unusually small or large, deformed structure, or heavily soiled eggs.

<u>Eggs on the Table for Ingestion</u>

To prevent embryo development or growth, gather quality eggs often—at least once a day. Take care when gathering to prevent any cracks that allow bacteria to enter and kill them. Wash and rinse washed eggs immediately after they have completely cooled off. Store unwashed eggs with the pointed end down at 55–65°F. Eat should be within 3–4 weeks of the lay date for maximum freshness and quality growing.

<u>Equipment for Handling Eggs</u>

To prevent damage, use egg baskets made of smooth type plastic or metal. For bigger operations or more eggs, egg cartoning machines can boost productivity.

For the best storage, choose for walk-in coolers or get industrial egg refrigerators. Egg washers with sanitizing chemicals might be profitable if you choose to use them for commercial sales. Quail eggs are best preserved when all handled carefully from the time of laying until they are stored or rounded incubated. This guarantees a steady supply of quail fresh eggs or hatching chicks for your operation's requirements.

Features of Quail egg

Quail eggs are quite smaller than chicken eggs, yet they are very more nutrient-dense and have a number of benefits over chicken eggs. They appeal to people who are health-conscious as well as those who are interested in cooking because of their unique in filled qualities.

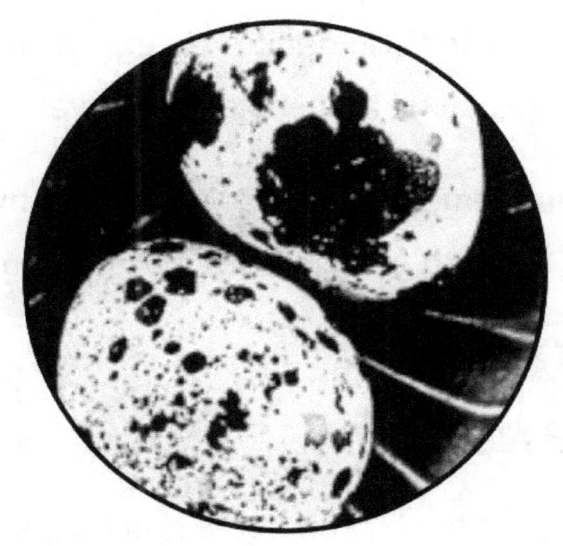

Profile of Nutrition

When quail eggs are then weighed against chicken eggs, they are:

• Higher in iron, riboflavin, protein, and other minerals, including vitamin B12.

• Greater levels of carotenoids and vitamin E, two advantageous antioxidants

Because diverse protein filled types make it easily digested for persons/humans with egg allergies, it has a lower overall fat and cholesterol level.

Portion management is made possible by their small size (10g-11g on average) and rich nutritious content.

Taste and Adaptability

When compared to chicken eggs, quail eggs have a much deeper face, almost nutty flavor. Their low ratio of weight to yolk offers:

• Outstanding emulsification qualities for sauces and dressings

• Offers a rich, creamy texture when cooked out

• Flavorful, vibrant orange-yellow yolks

• Enhanced taste for baked products, quiches, and other foods

Appeal to the Senses

Quail eggs have these tiny, speckled shells that are colored in cream, brown, blue, and green.

Decorative accent to made food plates; well-liked as whimsically colored Easter eggs; a unique touch to parties and eating occasions(you should have seen)

Simple to Make

When it comes to producing eggs from them, quail are significantly more productive than chickens for homes or even small farms. They can get earlier egg production at only 6–8 weeks old and the females laying up to 250-300 eggs yearly at peak

Part III: Advanced Quail Farming

CHAPTER 7: Housing and Facility Design

Large-scale Quail Housing Systems

Small quail flocks can be housed in your backyard coops, but housing systems for commercial operations need to be built for better efficiency and increased output quantities. To satisfy these needs, there are several large-scale quail house styles available to use

Systems for Battery Cages

A very effective commercial configuration makes use of small, multi-tier battery fixed cages

- Individual cages with feeders and nipple waterers hold eight to ten quail
- Slanted/vee-shaped flooring enable eggs to slide onto conveyor belts;
- Cages are organized in rows or tiers up to four levels high.
- Manure falls into a hole below wire flooring, making cleanup simple
- Offers a high stocking density of 1.2–1.45 square feet per adult quail.

Benefits of these cages include labor efficiency and maximum output per square foot.

Cons: Higher start-up expenses and steady worries about your animal welfare

Housing with Flat Decks

A different, higher-welfare strategy makes use of flat-deck housing:

- Nest boxes surrounding walls for egg-laying

- Feed/water lines run above with trough feeders/drinkers
- Low densities of birds kept in, 2-3 square feet per quail
- Continuous bed of litter or mesh wire flooring
- Manual or automated egg collecting conveyor

Benefits of these include reduced setup costs and more opportunities for their natural behaviors.

Cons: Requires more effort and produces fewer facilities.

Outdoor Pens and Runs

Simple outdoor pens or mobile pens/field shelters can all be effective for smaller operations:

- Capable of rotating pens throughout land to promote plant better regeneration
- Protected from any predators with appropriate fencing/netting guide

- Provided with additional housing structure with nest boxes and feeders
- Provided with access to sunlight and foraging places

Benefits: Excellent quail welfare and very inexpensive setup costs

Cons: Reduced output levels and seasonal difficulties

Ventilation, Lighting, and Climate Control

Sufficient ventilation averts the accumulation of any moisture and restores oxygen flowing around the cage;

The following features of negative pressure ventilation systems

- Inlet and exhaust fans, possible evaporative cooling pads

- Minimum ventilation rates of 0.7-1.0 CFM per pound of quail in.

Air mixing is facilitated by low air intakes and high exhaust fans in the space. Adequate fan sizing is required to provide the required air speed needed at quail level (450–600 fpm).

<u>*Luminance or lighting*</u>

For regular egg production and reproductive cycles, day length regulation is essential to offer them, here are the parameters for that;

- Light exposure of 16–18 hours promotes quality egg laying
- Dim-to-bright dimmers with automated timed lighting controls
- Light-emitting diode (LED) or fluorescent bulbs with 10–20 lux intensity

- Windows that let in some natural light are advantageous in the space for both you and your quail

Temperature Regulation

Although they can withstand some heat there, quail suffer more in very cold weather conditions.

- The optimal temperature range for manufacture is 65–85°F.

In the winter time, use brooders or hovers for extra warmth in the cage . In the summer, use high-speed set fans, evaporative cooling, and appropriate insulation passed through the cage space.

- Humidistat to keep relative humidity between 50 and 70 percent

Automation and Technology Integration

The integration of innovative technology and automated systems is becoming way more advantageous as quail farming enterprises expand in size, as it helps to maximize the production, profit gain or margins, and efficiency.

Environmental Regulators

Maintaining ideal climatic conditions to the last detail is essential to your quail success. Controls that are automated will smoothly govern :

- Air intake/exhaust and ventilation systems
- Temperature, humidity, and cooling
- Photoperiod and light dimming programs
- Water line and feed temperatures
- Centralized computer controls for the environment enable observation and modification

Feeding Mechanisms

Feeding is streamlined via automated spread feed handling and delivery to them

- Rigid/flexible auger systems for bulk feed conveyance
- Branch lines equipped with feed droppers and liquid dispensers
- Precisely portion and cycle feeding schedules
- Possible amalgamation with feed milling/batching

Water-Based Systems

It's important to provide a steady supply of pure clean, fresh water:

- Cup catchments on the lines of the breast feeders

Medicator tanks with automated flood defectors and flush cleaning cycles for vitamin and vaccination dispensing

Monitoring of water quality daily (chlorination, acidification, etc.) should be done regularly.

Manure Management

Efficient manure removal enhances better biosecurity and air quality around the coop.

- Conveyor systems or manure belt scrapers

Interfaces directly with composters or confinement areas; uses timed cycles or sensors to regulate the operation

Gathering and Managing Eggs

Optimize the quantity and quality of hatching eggs, if you want to use automated ways to transport them try out conveyors. If you have an egg keeping, fix a temperature controller in the room.

Data Management and Monitoring

Centralized monitoring and management of every area is made possible by integrated set computer systems; this set systems Sensors for the environment and equipment , monitors quail feed and water intake while also recording egg production and hatching information daily which totally helps manage your flock and maintain all records properly.

Large commercial quail operations benefit mostly from automation's longer-term labor reductions, better process controls, and more capabilities to find, despite its higher initial costs. Using intelligent technology in your farm maximizes output effectiveness.

CHAPTER 8: Quail Product Processing and Marketing

With your quail operation running all smoothly, the next step is preparing quail meat and quality eggs for sale while implementing effective marketing strategies we have proven to work and are willing to share with you. Proper processing, grading, packaging, and promoting your made products are essential for success.

Quail Meat and Egg Processing

Certain tools and methods are needed to process quail eggs and meat, the first meat processing is human regulated or shocked techniques of killing.

Evisceration lines with the potential to collect in organs and Scalding tanks or feather pickers. Grinders for meat and sausage for further processing

Egg Processing

- Sanitizing agent-equipped egg washers
- Conveyors and lights for inspection
- Egg oil applicators for bloom preservation
- Cold egg storage rooms
- Automated carton-ing and tray packaging

States and countries have different regulations regarding these licenses, area/facility standards, and food safety policies. Commercial sales often need **USDA/state(dep. of Agriculture)** inspections to work.

Grading and Packaging

Professional packing and consistent grading are essential for getting high-quality products.

- Meat Grading: Undergrad, poussin, and other size/weight categories
- Quality ratings according to flaws and fleshing

- **Egg grading**: - Graded according to size (mid, small, giant, etc.)
- Candled for blood/meat spots and air cells
- **Packaging**: Whole birds are packaged in vacuum like skins.
- Packaging that keeps frozen meats dry
- Egg cartons made of plastic, foam, or molded pulp
- Labeling with the necessary dietary information

For freshness of the whole products, a proper cold chain must exist in the farm from processing to delivery.

Strategies for Marketing and Sales

Emphasize the special nutritional advantages of your quail meat and eggs.

Encourage regional and sustainable brand positioning; Make use of eye-catching labeling design and branding, most quail farms don't Use online ordering and delivery, we tested it and found it has its way to reach a larger audience than a minimal quail farm.

Target upscale eateries and grocery shops; Go to food festivals and neighborhood gatherings around your area; you can also make use of influencer, big name and social media marketing in selling out.

CHAPTER 9: Management of Quail Enterprises

Budgeting and Financial Planning

As with any company successful venture, your quail farming operation's long-term survival and profitability depend solely on meticulous financial planning and budgeting. It's crucial to create accurate financial estimates and track success indicators.

Initial Expenses

- The cost of the land and facilities (processing areas, brooder barn, egg room, coops(house)
- Equipment, such as vehicles , feeders, drinkers, generators, and egg incubators.
- Foundation flock (supplier chicks or breeding stock)

- Bins for storing quail feed and the first delivery of feed
- First-year operating capital (feed, utilities, packaging, etc.)

Putting all of your beginning costs into a good budget enables you to look for sufficient funding for your growing business via loans, investors, etc.

Budgeting for Operations

Monitor both variable and fixed operational costs:

- Fixed: Marketing, insurance, equipment leasing, mortgages and rent
- Variables include labor, feed, utilities, packaging, and transportation.

Project revenue and cash flows

- Sales revenue estimates for meat, eggs, and chicks

- When income is compared to costs and loan payments

Maintaining a close eye on actual performance in comparison to your budget enables you to make necessary adjustments to each production levels or cost-cutting strategies.

Maintaining Records and Documentation

Tax compliance and the tracking of important performance indicators depend on the maintenance of thorough operational and financial records:

- Information on your flock management, like hatch rates, mortality level, and egg output.
- Production and sales figures for meat and eggs
- Bills for each and every expense
- Job records if employing personnel to take part

- Logged correspondence with inspectors and regulators

Rules and Legal

Now there are rules and legal considerations for owning a quail farm, there's Zoning and construction rules for your establishments, Licensing for commercial kitchens, meat processing, and whole agricultural activities

S/S/O/Ps, H/A/C/C/P, and food safety protocols if you are producing food for human consumption.

- Requirements for product labeling (codes, nutritional information, etc.)

- Environmental laws (air/water quality, manure or waste management, etc.)

- Employment rules (tax withholding, workers' monthly compensation, etc.) if you are employing labor to do the work.

Ensuring that you have the operational permissions, certificates, and total approvals required to do business correctly is ensured by consulting all legal specialists and regulatory bodies.

Part IV: Appendices

Appendix A: Quail Breed Profiles

The following appendix would provide more comprehensive biographies of the most widely used quail breeds that are commonly produced:

- Coturnix Quail, which includes Jumbo Brown, Tuxedo, and Japanese/Pharaoh.

- California Valley Quail - Bobwhite Quail

- Button Quail

The entry for each species might include:

- Origins and history
- - Physical attributes and standard descriptions
- - Normal weight intervals
- - Capabilities for producing eggs
- - Finish weights and meat characteristics
- - Personality and conduct characteristics

- Best when paired with color photographs

<u>Appendix B: Formulations for Quail Feed</u>

This would include example nutritional breakdowns and full feed formulas for them:

- ✓ Starter rations for chicks
- ✓ Develop/Grower Ratios
- ✓ Breeder/layer ratios
- ✓ Possible increases in calcium and protein in feed

Could provide an ingredient percentage list f0r quail feeds such as:

- ✓ Wheat, soybean meal, and corn
- ✓ Sources of fish or meat/bone meal
- ✓ Mineral and vitamin premixes

- ✓ Sources of large calcium, such as oyster shell or limestone

Appendix C: A Guide to Quail Health and Illnesses

A thorough simple manual that addresses health and common illness;

1. Bacterial illnesses (cholera, ulcerative enteritis, etc.)

2. Adrenal infections (NE, bronchitis, etc.)

3. Mycotoxin/fungus problems (aspergillosis, etc.)

4. Parasites (small worms, external parasite like lice, and coccidiosis)

Part V: Expert Quail Production

CHAPTER 10: Systems for Farming Quail

Pasture- and Free-Range Quail

Although enclosed housing and battery cage methods produce the most quail per square foot, more and more customers are requesting goods from free-range or pasture-based alternatives. The goal of these low-density type systems is to maximize outdoor access for any quail while also increasing animal wellbeing.

Unrestricted Quail

Quail in a free-range system have constant access to anything outside enclosures or runs throughout the day that offer:

- Locations for dust bathing themselves, foraging for food, and engaging in natural activities

- Having access to natural light or temperature, clean air, and outdoor settings

- Stress reduction via set vegetation and environmental enhancements

- Improved biosecurity through long-term outdoor enclosures

Simple coops or barns for nighttime security/protection, nest boxes, feeds, and other accessories make up proper housing. During the day, quail are free to roam as they wish between the outside enclosures and the housing.

Quail Raised in Pasture

Pasture-raised quail include actual rotational grazing over wide pastures, taking free-range idea to a whole new level. <u>Important components consist of:</u>

The ability to raise your quail in portable pens, bottom-less field type shelters, or tractors that are rotated on a regular basis;-Quail graze on grasses, forages insects, and vegetation of the pasture the grow on;-Manure coming from them naturally fertilizes and rejuvenates the land making it a win win.

Rules & Licensure

In order for goods to bear the labels "free-range" or "pasture-raised," farmers need to fulfill several requirements and guidelines we would detail out:

- ❖ Minimum specifications for outside access (run area lengths, number of hours per day, etc.)

- ❖ Maximums for space and density for interior dwelling elements
- ❖ Types of diet and supplementing restrictions
- ❖ Adherence to audits and standards for animal welfare in your region
- ❖ Organic certification procedures in the event that your quail is sold as organic

Free-range and pasture-raised quail goods do command premium pricing for their unique production claims since they involve way more effort and land to use. Adherence to all rules and meticulous planning of operations are necessary as well.

Farming Quail Organically

There has been a steady increase in consumer demand for organic items, such as quality eggs and chicken meat. Farmers that raise quail using approved organic farming methods/ways may diversify their crops and get higher prices when marketed proper. But following organic guidelines necessitates significant adjustments to a number of quail operations' components.

Requirements for an Organic System

To be eligible for organic certification, the following requirements need to be fulfilled before starting off:

Housing: Direct sunshine to the space and fresh air must be available to quail outside

Enough room must be provided for their natural behaviors like as dust bathing

Renewable and ecologically acceptable construction materials must be used in construction or coop or bird space.

Feed: Only components that have been certified organic are allowed to be fed. These include organic type grains, protein sources, minerals, and other supplements.

GMOs, artificial additives, fast growth promoters, or animal byproducts are not meant to be present.

- The possible feedstock use of agricultural wastes, such as bakery waste

Health Care: Vaccines are limited and examined on a case-by-case basis before given to them; most conventional drugs and antibiotics are outlawed, just make sure you check before giving them; only natural therapies and alternative cures are fully permitted; Preventative techniques than drugs , such as daily sanitization and low-stress

Processing: Particular guidelines for handling them, storing, and permitted treatments; Utilizing a tagged tracking system for packaging from farms to consumers (buyers)

Procedure for Organic Certification

It might take about two to three years to get the whole organic certification and entails:

1. Creating an Organic System Plan that includes every procedure

2. Creating a comprehensive good record-keeping system for the main audit trail

3. A three-year transition period for your land and facilities before obtaining any certification

4. Renewals and annual inspections conducted by a recognized certifying agency from the certification agency

5. Keeping buffer zones in place to avoid pollution coming in any way.

Organic quail farming is quite difficult yet profitable because of premium pricing and growing demand in these times. Planning is very necessary, nevertheless, because of the multi-year shift, increased input prices, challenges with health management, and strict regulatory adherence.

Many producers decide to begin by converting a little piece of their business at a time to full organic practices. A successful certification process depends on having appropriate needed paperwork and creating an approved Organic System Plan from the beginning.

Quail-Crop Systems Integrated

Quail-Vegetable Systems: - Quail are grazed in rotation across different vegetable patches or orchards; - Birds naturally ward off any harmful insects lying below and fertilize your plants; - Vegetation gives the birds extra fodder

Rotations of Quail-Field Crops: During fallow times, quail are then reared on crop leftovers or cover crops; prior to planting cash crops such as either maize or wheat, fields are fertilized with manure (which can also come from your quail

Advantages and Things to Think About

- ✓ Less need on synthetic herbicides and fertilizers in your farm

- ✓ Improved component-to-component nutrient cycling all around

- ✓ Diversified revenue streams from various items in the farm

Rules and Certifications for Quail Farming

Quail farming enterprises are subject to a whole number of federal, state, and municipal laws, while being on a smaller scale than bigger poultry companies. Furthermore, certain optional certificates might be valuable additions incase, but they demand strict! adherence to predetermined guidelines. Any lawful quail or agricultural company must comprehend and comply with these regulations.

❖ Regulatory Supervision

The following government organizations are in charge of quail farm regulation:

USDA/APHIS: in charge of keeping an eye on all biosecurity protocols, illnesses affecting your poultry, and laws govern any interstate transportation in poultries which registration is necessary.

FDA/State Dept. of Agriculture: If you are manufacturing goods for human consumption enforce food safety laws such as H/A/C/C/P protocols. Inspections and licenses can be necessary as time goes on.

EPA/State Environmental Agencies: Control the use of using pesticides and pharmaceuticals, permits for air and water discharge, in your area and the management of manure.

OSHA/Labor Departments: Workplace safety regulations, especially or mostly for agricultural processing plants.

Local Municipal Authorities: They are responsible for enforcing local area laws; building or giving permits, zoning regulations, and water use rights.

Label Claims and Certifications

Apart from just ensuring regulatory compliance, optional certifications facilitate the promotion of distinctive value propositions.

Organic: Requires two or more years of adherence to organic agriculture me standards and is administered by full certified certifying agencies.

Nutritional Labeling: Claims about nutrients for product packaging that have been approved based on inspection or lab examination.

Although some small producers are not subject to any restrictions, expansion often leads to heightened scrutiny.

CHAPTER 11: Management of Quail Enterprises

Strong business management abilities are quite necessary for a quail operation to run well, even beyond just quail husbandry. Long-term sustainability and profitability depend heavily on careful record-keeping, careful financial planning as we said earlier, and compliance with laws and regulations.

Budgeting and Financial Planning

Whether you are running a huge commercial quail farm or it's just a tiny home business, creating thorough financial predictions is very crucial.

- ❖ Initial Expenses

1. Land/facility expenses (for better processing spaces, egg keep rooms, and coops)

2. Equipment, such as bird feeders, generators, cars, and incubators.

3. Foundation flock (chickens or the breeding stock)

4. Storage area for feed and first delivery of feed

5. Operating capital to cover costs for the first year of starting

Here are all we looked at before starting our quail farm and promise you it worked well.

Budgeting for Operations

- Monitor all your fixed expenses like as marketing, insurance, and mortgage/rent.

- Variable expenses (labor or workers, bought feed, utilities, packing, etc.)

Project sales income from your farm should commonly come from meat, quality eggs, and chick's sale.

Now here a whole advice that has proven to work if you own or willing to start your own quail farm, success on your endeavors, we hope this book meets what you looking for.

THANK YOU

RECORD PAGE

NOTE

www.ingramcontent.com/pod-product-compliance
Lightning Source LLC
Chambersburg PA
CBHW071936210526
45479CB00002B/700